THIS DIRTY
LITTLE HEART

A Lynx House Book

EASTERN WASHINGTON
UNIVERSITY PRESS

THIS DIRTY
LITTLE HEART

b. t. shaw

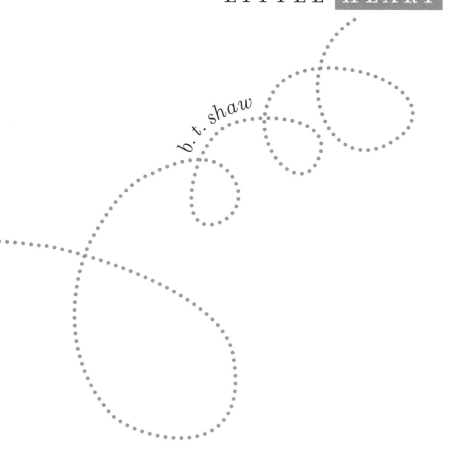

14   13   12   11   10   09   08   5   4   3   2   1

Cover art: Andrea Benson, *Life Saver* (2006)

Cover and interior design by A. E. Grey

Library of Congress Cataloging-in-Publication Data

Shaw, B. T. (Brenda T.)
  This dirty little heart / B. T. Shaw.
      p.   cm.
  "A Lynx House book."
  Includes bibliographic references.
  ISBN-13: 978-1-59766-040-2 (alk. paper)
  I. Title.
  PS3619.H3917T47 2008
  811'.6—dc22

                                                           2007050537

Eastern Washington University Press
Spokane and Cheney, Washington

For Wil, John, and Molly

CONTENTS

This dirty—little—Heart
Is freely mine.
I won it with a Bun—
A Freckled shrine—

But eligibly fair
To him who sees
The Visage of the Soul
And not the knees.

[Emily Dickinson]

I'm not entirely displeased
with the shirt front.

[Paul Cézanne]

THE IMPORTANCE OF FINGERS
IN A RHETORIC OF GESTURE

Tree monkeys raised me.
Glorious slack-hammock arms!
Fur like hashish fog.

HUNGER

tuesday's dinner for five
was noodles with noodles
baked in ketchup

night before that
squirrel dredged like chicken
stuck in the oven

last of the winesap jam
mold scraped from its wax cap

little sister plays
with salt-stuffed tails
says *mink stoles*

at school heads go down
on the art-room table

the sharp knife makes a pigeon
stretch five ways

red clay clay birds bird shot
morels dogs on scent
wild ginseng night-gigging

we keep some things
to ourselves

hold those names
in our soft mouths

NO. 2 VENUS

Sophomore English I spent
diagramming Inez

      hair like summer dusk
soft cedar shaded weighted
strands of light so thick I was sure
some had tried but none
not even golden Bobby Esselstein
had grabbed it all grabbed grabbing
in some back seat

my mouth busy with the mistake
end of a pencil
grainy pink rubber and metal
ringing on fillings and tongue
thin yellow paint
(most poisonous part)
red wood yielding under my teeth

      full glossed lips that made it impossible for her
not to lean over and say
to any available boy
Lend me a dollar? I'm flat
busted
arching her eyebrow and blue beauty mark
when he answered the pluperfect curve
of her sweater

my left hand stretched to the edge of my desk
hoped hoping hope
for Inez to toss back her hair
let it land on my fingers
conjugate miracles
for the dishwater blonde
the chicken-legged

       and the last day of school
Inez in the girls' room
dabbing beige makeup
over the blue mark
under her eyebrow
to cover to hide
said to no one
said certainly never to me
said *Damn him*
One more inch and I'd be blind

I could see it then
little tail in a hand
blue graphite snapped off
under the skin of a noun of a person
place object or thing
to brand to tattoo *Things happen*
things happen things
happen to you

IMAGES IN ANSWER TO BIOLOGY

Flocked birds in an agar sky.

Pulley. Scale. Skeleton—
stick-flippered, penis-boned—
mid-stroke at the ceiling.

Boy by the door: *I was late as a fish.*
Spectacled girl: genus humanitas.

Can I get everyone's attention this way?

Lines of magnetic force. Bunsen
burner. Loaded inoculating loop.

WE BRING THE WRONG TOOLS

and find ourselves unprepared
for sky's grip on the white pine.
Handsaw. Shovel. Nylon rope
in my gloved hands. My father saws
an hour into heartwood before stopping,
breathless, to lean. I offer to take up the saw.
He refuses, he always refuses—he doesn't trust
chance. So we break, he recounts a lifetime
of severed trunks: redbud, sycamore, a hemlock
that tried to crack his nine-year-old skull—

The tree still stands, my father won't rest,
grips the resined handsaw in his right fist,
presses his will with his left, but it is the third
fist that strikes me, rapid flex in his barrel chest,
predictable, terrible, so when the pine finally yields

I am blind to the work, the guide rope rips
through my hands and between us the trunk
twists momentarily
unstoppable.

APIARY

Older, eleven, she took me outside
her mother's house—mango tangled

in torch ginger, avocado, palm.
I'll show you how it's done—

Through air thick enough to wear,
bees rumbled their vernacular

of threat and need, pollen-coated,
and when one slid down an angel

trumpet's throat, my guide's slick hand
shot out and sealed the floral envelope,

yanked it from the stem—

Pure instinct in a fist, the insect
pitched inside the flower's lipsticked

kiss, a momentary prize we shook—
a little hot maraca, stinging rattle—

which later, bored, we smacked
and burst against the rock steps to her house

where—combed, culotted—our mothers
thrummed among the compound eyes.

LICKING COUNTY: 1931

She poses, perched atop her mother's split-
rail fence. Laughing, presses big-boned
thighs into his slight and suited knees.
He smiles back, bends his head
away from her, one elbow thrust
beyond the camera's frame, his fingers
furling in his lap. Her arm is fast
around his neck, her hand a clutch

of narcissi as though she didn't think
she stood a chance with lace of Anne
or wild lilac, heady, lush and drunk.
As though she'd never know the patience
of the paper birch, would never look
like hazel blooming witchlike in the snow.

PORTRAIT OF MY GRANDFATHER
AS RHETT BUTLER

Frankly, my dear,
I don't give a darn.

AND WHEN I HEAR THAT VOICE
I FEEL A GREAT JOY

They say it doesn't strike twice. But lightning is plural.
A chorus. One hundred touches per second. One hundred
tales in illegible cursive—each particular

           as a girl in a crowd, my mother,
maybe, seeking relief from afternoon heat
close as skin. Hand over hand

in LaSourdesville Lake, out to a water-bound
merry-go-round—metal rod circled with rings—
from which children would twirl, swing, spin
into thin moments of flight, releasing to arc
beyond gravity's hand, thrill in the pause
before falling. That day

        the sky darkened, my mother ignored voices
from shore. And here

        my grandmother wades into the story, hitching
her skirt, dragging her daughter to shelter, both lit
with anger. And lightning—

that liar—

        struck twice, arcing the merry-go-round.
Two touches. One body. She washed to the shore,
another twelve-year-old girl who believed she could ride
out the storm. My mother

stood by the side of a pool in the rain,
telling this story. *Charred*, she said, and I felt it,
a fulgurite under my skin. Path of lightning—
through grandma, my mother, a stranger, myself.

I've heard church bells in France once sang
to scare away lightning. Even then, in an ocean
of polled wood, a girl—

lifting her eyes to the harrowing sky,
waiting for voices.

FIELD NOTES ON THE FAMILY

rabbit brush   alfalfa
  bright blue narrow
pair of grasping

                            slender   wings
              little known, seldom

from each other
          months given   erroneously considered
families comprise groups of

                 [indistinct darker margins]
          in a variety of sites

PHYSICAL LAW

A body in motion stays in motion.
Pushed, a spinning object pushes back.

Yes—but when our teacher claimed
lead and feathers fall at equal rates

(in worlds without resistance), you said
she wasn't right. You couldn't be convinced.

By twelve, you'd seen enough to know how hard
some things can hit. I should've asked—

more than once I lay in bed across the street,
heard him throw his voice against the night.

At rest, not every body rests. The proof
was you. A falling man accelerates

like stone: pushed, a girl will fly
apart like rain.

HUBERT, N.C.

It was an economy of Bills and blue notes
wrung from the smoke of bleached men
who trawled for Zingo's Fish House
and bristle-nobbed boys from base wanting

for a while the world in a girl behind a hip-high rail,
wearing short of nothing glossed in Midnight Pearl
Maybelline and the twitch of daylight law
that after dark got down to legally actionable
anatomical detail, prohibited contact
but couldn't account for the lasting impact
of two-thousand-square-pounds-pressure
per—what else?—stiletto heel—

on tendons, soles, the pocked linoleum floor
between the living and the making of it, less or more.

THE PAST IN THIRTEEN PRESENTS

[1] Cowgirl getup (red hat, red skirt, red vest with white fringe),
including cap gun in tooled holster: basement, [residence],
Worthington, Ohio, in box near oscilloscope

[2] Two-wheeler (red) with handlebar streamers; inaugural ride
in light snowfall: garage, ibid.

[3] Charm bracelet (faux-turquoise totem pole, hatchet, Arizona
in silhouette): Public Storage, Portland, Oregon, cardboard
whisky box

[4] Bone-china miniature, palomino (from C.S., then twelve:
"Your face is pretty from the eyes up"): op. cit. n. 1 (note:
missing right foreleg)

[5] Patent leather go-go boots (white), size 4: whereabouts
(regretfully) unknown

[6] Simulated-topaz ring (10k-gold–filled): [residence],
Columbus, Ohio, backyard, perhaps behind boxwood hedge

[7] Made-in-Taiwan porcelain lovebirds (pair): sold, 25 cents
each, garage sale; op. cit. n. 2

[8] *The Road to Ensenada* (cassette), Lyle Lovett: last seen
inside X's black-handled valise, backseat, rusted-out VW
Rabbit, Emerald Isle, N.C.

[9] Lace-trimmed underthings (lavender): scissored, set alight; kitchen sink, [residence], ibid.

[10] Frying pan: flung, cornfield, Interstate 90, Kansas; cf. ante

[11] Abacus: bookshelf, beside sparrow skull unearthed in the garden that spring (when digging seemed the only way to count again): [residence], Portland, Oregon

[12] Breakfast, viz., hot oats, raisins, fireweed honey: sleeping bag on ledge, North Rim, Grand Canyon National Park, Arizona; nota bene

[13] Paper (red as cardinal wings): ibid., ibid., ibid. et passim

THE FIRST TIME YOUR DAUGHTER
RUNS AWAY FROM HOME

a fryer sits in the kitchen half butchered, its legs akimbo.
A glass of ice water sweats on the dining room table. Who
left that there? What time is it? When did you quit smoking?
A phone in the hand is worth nothing. You sit at the window,
the sun sinks below your neighbor's roof. Someone else's kid

kicks a rock up the street in the gathering dark, his legs carrying
him home. You don't know him. You wish he were missing.

There are sentences you can start but you can't say
what she's wearing, your daughter, that little stitch in your side.
Seed pearl, loaded die. You wonder how you might bargain
with a god to whom you aren't speaking.

Her friends and the friends of her friends, no one knows
or no one is telling, and the argument this morning about the boy,
oh boy, the boyboyboyboy. You held your ground, you thought
you'd gotten through, but in tonight's light you see you were
more naked than you knew. You wanted to shake her, to hold her,
you wanted, you want, and now the clock

has the only hands in the house
that know what to do. Moths flock to the porch light.
A bowl of grapes waits in the refrigerator.

And when it's no longer late dinner but predawn,
a shadow you recognize crosses the lawn, her feet raising a drift
of fallen cherry blossoms that were—as it turned out this time—

only mimicking winter.

SYMPATHETIC RESPONSE

The sun turns to paste after two. Everything sticks—
cracker crumbs, tree muzz, kids. Dried bits
of what's past. Mornings you write to-do lists

on your wrist—nights, wash them into
the garden's cracked mouth. Late August,
yellow jackets frantic, brains squeezed

to BBs by kiddie pools, BBQs, seasonal
suspicion: odds of surviving intact.
See that slab patio

                out back? That's where
later you'll think you've stepped on a sliver
of glass, pull up short to pick out the shard,

find a catch: fighting winged thing
attached with both butt end and nippers.
You'll not yelp—(that's instinct: you live

among nappers)—but will flap ten fingers,
flail in tight circles, then smother, smash,
grind into the grass *cuticle* and *mandible*—

words rushing onto the scene from a show
the children watch (antic, lean, the science guy
could be your brother). When it's long past dead,

you'll stop and, foot in hand, consider
the once-fending thing. Thorax. Quieted
head. One dismembered wing. Another.

The lab-coated man in your brain pan
will cough up *carapace* and *do not bother the queen*—
while your histamined synapses sing—

it stings like a mother.

REHEARSAL NOTES FOR ADOPTIVE MOTHER

1. FORGIVE MY STATING THE OBVIOUS

So, in the beginning you weren't thinking
about foreshadowing and compound views.
That took years, though eventually you happened
on the multiplex as organizing tool: three stories

shot and looped, showing independently
to mixed reviews. That's you, your girl, and a third
neither of you knew. Scene 422: The day after
the first day she ran away, she's on the stoop:

always with that third, that steadfast ghost
of Mother No. 2. Listing all the ways
you'll never do, including, though not limited to,
the fact (she blinks at you) the fact of what it was

you stole (not what the other couldn't keep).
Subtext: *Living with you makes me want to puke.*

You think but do not say: *What I took,*
if anything, it was for granted the difference

I might make—while she concentrates
on grinding down the toebox of one shoe,
the rubber or what passes for it nowadays
marking hashes on the concrete strip—

a sound a Foley artist might replace
with something like the *shhh* a woman makes
to soothe a child. It's the middle of the day—
you're in the dark.

                        Well, you say, *I*—
(hand across her hair)—*let's go inside*—
though you're no longer sure the door
is imperceptibly ajar.

Here all week the rain has washed the yard.
Into the street. Daffodils gone jaundiced.
Peonies a sodden pink that tastes like chalk.
Even in the dark. Moonlight sprawls across.
The bed like a hexed dog, while the downpour.
Paints a temporary portrait on the roof.
À la Seurat. It's spring. The world's pushing.
Its point afresh. A rush of green-pronged growth.
Campaigns to square things up, pin stuff down.
In magnificent vectors. The neighborhood's good.
Mothers are asleep, you're sure, welcome.
In the temporary land of unbecoming. But you.

Lie awake—some nights you find the alphabet.
In reverse a shibboleth, so Z, Y, X, you work.
Your way to A. Rinse. Repeat. There's no rest.
For the wicked or the weary. Either way.
The past is past the point of no return.

Still you keep coming back to the start.
Of her. Your daughter. The way you tell.
It to yourself at night. *A woman*.

Walked into a bar. The bartender asked.
What'll it be? The remainder written.
On your girl's face. In varying degrees.
Of indecipherable Greek.

This morning's clue—a photo of her flutters from a book
she hucked weeks ago at you and missed, spine splayed since
in a kitchen corner. Skirt hiked to her hips, arms flung
above her head—she's in some stranger-to-you's brass twin bed.

She's fourteen, there's frost on the street, without you
your brain tries to figure what it'd cost to turn up the heat.
Mystery of the 99 Steps. In a chair your three-legged dog
paws the air, chasing in his sleep a bicycling squirrel

of prodigious intellect and size. The mail: gathering
in the hall since June. The vacuum: permanent addition
to the living room. You: trapped in amber ordinariness.
These last few weeks you've come to understand

the object's role in *motherfucked*—though mostly
you sit, another decaf at your wrist, ticking through
a list of what you did and should have done.
The novel's perky girl detective gazes

up at you as though there's something hidden
in your face. In seventh grade, your reading teacher
scratched a line through *titian-haired* in your required
book report, docking points. Her ink was red—

that's funny now—though you'd spent hours then,
failing to suss out where you'd gone wrong. Jesus—
you're fundamentally unprepared for this, this
whoop-de-do, this what-have-you. At your girl's age

your gender was librarian—how should you
know what to do? What would Nancy Drew do?
No note, no hidden panel in the clock,
no wind-up doll, no locked box—

           outside the kitchen window,
a fox squirrel flicks its tail for counterpoise
and leaps—branch to fence to street, landing
(*the dog growls in his sleep*) on its feet.

If you could make her listen to you now
you'd tell her how you wanted her so much
you wished on stars. Predictably, the moon.
But also moths, sticks, spoons. Traffic lights.

And the faulty range-top burner. Two clicks
to ignite, she'd be here soon—three meant
sooner. Four and the miniature giants
in your head would take their cues and tap

across the nightly parallax of what might be.
You didn't know you'd never sleep the same again—
the way you slept before your brain conceived
of her. If you'd known then—

the limits of the best intentions, your own
volition (*that dream—taking off the coat again,
again to find its double underneath*)—
contradictions of this dirty little heart—

you want to say none of it would matter.
She's your daughter. Not flesh of your flesh,
true, but bone chip of your compound fracture,
and vice versa—neither of you who you were

before the other. That last thing, you can't—
it's nothing she would want to hear.
But for when again she's anywhere
that's near, have at hand an offhand

How've you been?
meaning it to mean—

You were a toddler in red shoes. I took
one look and knew I'd be a goner.

It's a late October Wednesday, the anniversary
of her entrance at the small gray house—
grounded ghosts of maple leaves swirling
in the drive. She was not yet two when she arrived.
Her quilted coat was pink—the only word
she used was no. Still you hefted her—she rode
on your back through the open door.

This day the maple's paper hands whisk
in uselessness against the dry-stack wall.
It might be lonelier without the loneliness,
it's been said—weeks missing, your voice
gone hoarse, and no real word
for the shape an absence takes.

Now what's fallen must be raked—
what's not, made ready for the freeze.
Under a windswept pile of leaves you find
a thing with feathers the cat has tried
and failed to swallow whole. Done in,
done to—long after curtains draw,
you'll still be trying to decide—

what's left—what's right to leave
exactly as it lies.

BY NOW NO DOUBT

You'd think we'd be inured to fall—
maple red, walnut yellow—but undeterred
we talk the way we always talk

this time of year, with some degree
of postlapsarian surprise. As though
words could slow the set gears

of the world. Prone in other seasons
to reflection, the pond has grown
thin-skinned and droll, its shore

flocked with cattail fur and frost.
A fattened pack of adolescent geese
has leveraged the lawn: leaving is not lost

on them. Their unrehearsed infinitives
hover on the pond—instinct seems
an enviable gift. They'll rise with it

eventually, above the dog's alarm,
pulled from day's short reach
and—on a wing—be gone.

REVISIONARY

A sudden blow. The great wings beating still—
till Leda balls her fist, splits
the motherfucker's bill.

ONE MORE NAME
YOU WON'T ASSOCIATE WITH WATER

A vacation was, he said, the next logical step—
brochures boasting 90-pound halibut,
snapper, sole, something called chocolate chip
fish that must have been named by a latent optimist
or handicapped god, a challenged oculus.

What followed was defined by what he reeled in
from the surf: skates with scalpel tails; innumerable
undersized flounder; two agave-spined grouper
with eyes like dried glue, bodies hermaphroditic
and small. But it was the unriled shark
that made you a verified mystic—flash
of tail, skin iridescent. He fixed it for supper.

You tasted urine, grit, a hole dug in the Mojave.

AFTER A FASHION

> *Brown is the new black.*
> [*Glamour* magazine]

Red is the new pink. Pink is the new blue.
Magenta's excuse is yesterday's news,
and sources agree the new neutral
is puce. Lavender is the new beige, sienna
the new sage. What about spruce? Caught
burnt-umber-handed, thwackingly drunk,
attempting to board Air Force One.
Apprehended by green, the new tangerine.

Do you remember that night at the Alibi Lounge?
Scarlet was the new white, white the new news—
that was years ago. We danced, your hands
in my hair. Black light turned the gin indigo.

SOLO

Arched against the murmurs of the crowd,
the saxophonist leans. A beat—he seems to hold

the moon, halved by argument, aloft.
Tempered slice. Cleanly cut.

(Do you remember what we fought about?)

The note bends, breaks like boughs or limbs or luck.
(I recollect: nick of moon, my teeth against your back.)

Like circuitry. Or dawn. The pause
the player straightens in. Silence.

Poppies of applause.

IT GOES WITHOUT SAYING

                              Damp larcenies
of mouth and breath. Two stories down:
tall drink of a man in leather and a blonde
in Byron's boots who leans against
a third of some distracted gender.
The signal turns,

                    we watch them cross,
swim out of view—as later we will, too,
though not now, holding, holding,
on the planet with the wrong name,
strangers in us waiting for their cues.

WE END, LIKE GALILEO

With years came diminishing ability to focus
on objects at hand. Pen nib. Collar stud.
Ruby nest of squab bones on a dinner plate.

Behind, then, the distance failed.
Northern hills and eastern olive groves
lost ground until the vineyards vanished
in soft wash of green chintz and gold silk.

He charted each loss in its sidereal arc.
Until the tipped stars, too, emptied the glass,
opening the curtain on everyday dark.

EVEN EVE

A slut—then he slammed the door on her,
                        apple-cheeked, in Tulsa,
bird-with-head-cut-off flapping spastically
                        behind the pinched rib.
Cain by then unable (experts correlating
                        his behavior to maniac
DNA), Abel caned. House foreclosed,
                        Impala impounded, and
Eros too whacked on smack to leave them
                        anything but sore.
Flesh abundant yet still unfitting: who'd imagined
                        so much self?
God—her fingers worried the sofa's bouclé tweed.
                        Who'd get the dog?

Honey, the narrator said, he don't want no dog—
                        man's got a new yen. Oh,
if I were twenty years younger and unstained,
                        the sofa sobbed. If I
jibed instead of jabbed, the sterling chimed.
                        If I danced like Debi J.,
knobs out to here, the credenza cried.
                        To no reply. The bogus bonk
laid out in daylight—she saw how blind she'd been.
                        Suspect speed-dial?
Madam L., Next-Best Western. Account skimmed
                        to scum? Adam,
not error. Eve'd believed: the hangovers,
                        torn unders, lost button.

One and one makes three, the narrator nattered.
                    Add it up, take no
parts from the whole. No sign too bright to ignore,
                    no bag too big to strap,
Q-tip, on your back. No transmission too dropped
                    for that devil in Pit Q,
rot being the root—*Shut your head,* Eve said.
                    She was plotting each factor:
sex, sloth, wrath, that whole buffet. Saccharine.
                    Hummers. Quick nitro fixes.
Ten commandments, got it, but what to do
                    at eleven? fingerlings in fishnet,
urge to eat everything à la mode all-consuming,
                    dialogue diminishing (e.g., *RU
vulcan? i<3 rubber*). Infinite wisdom on the line,
                    they'd dashed for almanac luv.

Was it the snake, then, or the snacks?
                    Who knew. They came, they saw
X marked a spot, they concurred, they bought, dug in,
                    fell out, shorts in a helix.
You bobbed unthinking, the narrator thought, sure someone
                    would toss a girl a buoy.
Z' plane, z' plane! the dog persisted—on the y axis,
                    Eve making fast for a sloe-gin fizz.

FORGETTING MAY BE PART
OF THE PROCESS OF REMEMBERING

inhibiting the encroachment, say,
of the word *sky* on the word *cielo*—

or the elevator stopping short
of our floor the night we called it a day.

Boning knife inside a tackle box—
(*mano nella mano*) how it

tenderly slips fin from skin, egg sac
from any future without a pan.

What made me run my thumb one time
lengthwise across the blade—the blood—

but where was I? Doubling back,
about to talk about the weather

an ocean away—how clouds veil
the early winter moon with no risk

of touching. *Sei/sono*/you are/I am
(*without you*) beside myself, head full

of things I can't put a finger on.

NEW MATH

This is long division. This is not happily ever
after. Together comes apart to get her

the kitchen table, bath towels, not-so-easy chair.
(He takes the sofa, bookshelf, toaster,

and the name.) He'll be forever
bodied for her in the mingled scents of after-

shave and morning coffee made before
the thrash of back to bed. She tries to sever

certain ties, pants, shirts from the core
of corollaries: the recumbent his and hers. Where

his clothes once hung, a cipher
fills the closet that they share—

no, that conclusion's incorrect, she for-
gets to carry *d*—the word, after

all is said and done, is *shared*. One letter
difference and difference is what's left: matter

that refuses to agree, the prime denominator
of the fairy tale—one divided into ones and not a pair.

TERRA FIRMA BLUES

There's no light left to lose at four ayem.
So, tell me, what dog-bone note—
what tide, what bruise—I bartered
for this monochrome paint box
filled with hypertrophic wounds
and jelly moons? Like you,

like anyone awake, I have some things
I'd like to navigate, play out. I've got
all night—please show me how
to briefly duck the devil's one good eye.
Exactly what to slip him while his hands—
luminous and watertight—keep time.

MOST ACCIDENTS OCCUR AT HOME

You threw water on grease fires.
Tripped on the lip of the tub. At night,
alone, you think you smell smoke
in your hair. Hear a voice raised

like a fist—
Like so, you say to yourself. *Like this*.

Forgive yourself, sifting ashes for facts:
twisted buckles, heat-sobered knives,
anniversary photo in which you are caught
forever off guard, ready to strike a match.

SPRING COMES TO THE MISTRESS OF THE OBVIOUS

Iridescence replaces winter's aerodynamics—
tripped, hooked, a fantastic arrow
rammed in the marrow. Dawn lands
like an uppercut—nothing like you.

I've forgotten last March. And May
promises to blur as soon as I clear
moth-eaten silks from the drawer.
How wonderful it is this time of year

to not be in love. Outside, the ducks
resume a violet shouting, malachite
drakes hitting dun-colored targets,

the cads inflaming the pond, disturbing
(*not me, not me*) brackish water,
air-encumbered light.

MARGIN OF ERROR

For example, she says, take
the supercontinent Gondwana, pulled twice
out of Earth's mantle only to finally draw
and quarter itself after breeding an arkful
of hyperthyroidized lizards, flightless cranes,
and a species of fish with no jaw.

She keeps a list. Penicillin.
Ptolemy's failure to save appearances.
West Saharan fossils of footed cetaceans.
The late-night meteorologist's predictions.
And her heart. Though at times—
Meanwhile. Obviously. Night.

THE INVISIBLE WOMAN VS. MR. FANTASTIC

Honey, she said, *it's not your fault.*
I saw everything in you except myself.

TO AVOID UNNECESSARY DEATH

heed the rattler's warning.
Its tightly coiled rasp,

the burr, the catch, the purr
emptied of its chance of cat.

A brindled sound. Rapid slap. Hunting
once my uncle's half-mutt Appaloosa reared,

nostrils dilated, synapses flared, she struck
the gravel trail and, shrieking, thrashed

a gem-backed length of garden hose,
somebody's trash. Passion may be blind—

truth hisses in the ear. Click of teeth. Snap
of sheets. Kitchen door just before it's latched.

STATE OF THE STATE OF AFFAIRS

Not a dream but a fragment set loose again, splitting the night
    again.
Lavender and lemon verbena—gone when you turn on the light
    again.

The *Kama Sutra* demands an elegant woman know sixty-four
    points.
To begin: *A cockfight ain't over till one rooster dies—or can't rise to
    fight again.*

Blue list: empty pool, single shoe, last gushing letter (unsent).
Last time your child falls asleep in your arms. The hope she
    might again.

If a personnel carrier leaves Camp Lejeune at 5:24 and steams
    east until dawn,
would you find me this time in Paris? No answer makes the past
    right again.

ABSENT-MINDED

The pea was gone. And yet the princess
never slept the same again.
Each night

           fresh bruises bloomed
when she turned out the light, forget-me-
nots in ribbons on her shoulders, hips,
the soft *c* where the backbone grips the rib.
Or notes in minor keys across her wrists
and lids, as though her dreams were inked
and leaked. Years

          naturally went by. Faced with facts,
she opted to believe it was nothing

           that she felt. A sharp
but hollowed spot—like the pea but not.
Like what is left in linen by a moth
or careless match. A run, she came to think,
in a stocking—

          which, by definition, must be nothing
to be something. Like a point in space behind
a pebble that's been thrown. Or this:
the pressure of a finger that's let go.

BOY WITH GOOSE

Feet spread to brace against, the marble boy—
moon-faced, struck—grips the upstretched neck

of a bird in need of flight. Mouth wide with fright,
she can't twist her face far enough to bite. His glee

knows no consequence. A kind of screwy grace,
his ignorance (the road to hell before it's paved).

I love this goose so much! the unlined mouth insists—
while the fists can't stop stopping what they can't save.

LIKE THIS, ONLY MORE SO

In the Algarve, white stucco chimneys
like abandoned dollhouses.

From vents, smoke's ephemeral language.
A bottle of wine, a white dress, a rooftop patio.

Across a sky with bougainvillea clouds, racing pigeons
swerved en masse toward Banco Espírito Santo.

I watched you watching the birds—your face
turned as they reeled at a whistle. For a moment,

the full glass in my hand was filled and, in my hand,
full and made of glass.

WHAT WE MADE

we made from water and Spiderman comix.
Midden, maidenhair fern, cinnamon tic-tacs.
Screws from my mini-calculator. Belts
from your busted alternator.

      In Cerveteri, we made it from subterranean asters
and Lawrence's gentians. In Lisbon, marionette wire,
Sacher torte and suspicion. And that weekend
at Deception Pass—the supernumerary stars turning
out to be nothing but spindled construction paper
and a fluorescent bulb. I relied on gray wool—
remember? and you on two pennies rubbed together.
So in the end—

      I don't know. We had something
like a dog and pony show. But for a dog,
you might say, if I could tell you. And a pony,
you could count on me to remind you.

TO THE EX-HUSBAND'S NEWBORN:

You are the child of my discontent—

the possibility of you conceived in a stalled car
outside a strip mall stereo store, your father and I
biting into one last fight, unwilling or unable
to hear each other anymore. We took the fall
for you.

Funny now, looking back at the things
that made room for you: Mismatched
socks. A half-finished kitchen. And rows
of leggy blue lake beans, the bindweed
winding through the yellowed leaves,
sibyl blooms mouthing *O, O, O—*

O, kin to my children. O, daughter
not my daughter. Though I know
I'd do it all again: I wasn't meant
to be your mother.

Still, tonight, holding you I wished
for something other—some role
language has no word for. To be to you
an undertone or consolation prize.
A once-removed. Not a given, but made,
with luck,

close enough for comfort.

AFTERMATH

In this frame you are four, you have learned:
one plus one—that's two. One house
with aluminum siding, one brother
off-kilter beside you. One fence, one
view, one tree and its one, two, too many
fallen leaves, falling. Your scarf's a singular red.
Coat: unremarkable plaid. One sky, one
yard, one mother—she's pressing the shutter.
Gloved hands at your chest, you smile.
The wind numbers the hairs on your head.

But years have gone by and the boy in that shot
is a cracked rock in reverse, mended by thaw.
He's you subtracted, minus some number
of squared fists and circular thrashings. You
before nights spent driving through fire,
left lung cramped to make room for the heart.
Before gauging the difference one makes, before
gathering the losses it takes to split false spring
from true, what to carry from what to count on.

PUT THOU MY TEARS INTO THY BOTTLE

After everything unthinkable was thought
then done—Sodom gone, daughters
unnamable and damned—Lot packed
his wife in silica and shipped her to America
to retire in Seattle. For the waters—

the nine-times-forty days of rain
that turned the world more shades of green
than he could count. In the apartment garden,
her body wept all winter, dwindling from pillar
to something slightly larger than a grain of salt.
At her feet among the ferns, the tears fell into pails.

Come spring she filled the small aquarium—he imagined
she was rushing through the heart of the albino eel
or swimming in the red-lipped blenny's eyes.

Each night he prayed he'd glimpse her in the tank.
But she'd grown quick and wouldn't let him catch her
looking back.

WINGING IT

This morning, I woke ninety miles from you
as the crow flies. This cabin sits a stone's throw
from a creek, which, from bank to bank, could not
be more than thirty salmon wide. The water's slow
but cold, and I can't reach the other side. I tried.
I'm ninety miles from you as the crow flies.

Which may be more like forty-five as jackdaws wing.
A steady rain has veiled the distant shore
since noon, and I can't keep the woodstove lit.
(If I say *blue*, do you see *lips*?) What's more,
I slipped and soaked my boots—I'm stuck inside.
Just sixty miles from you as magpies slide.

But more like thirty-one as the wind blows—
and what in horsefly miles I'll never know.
I'm oceans from you as the mermaids sing.
Mere micrometers as the mountains grow.
Rain falls in sheets—the distance seems too much.
Yet you're just half a mile away as woodchucks chuck.

If the clouds should clear, the Milky Way will stun
the sky tonight, and light will fall from stars
long fallen in their fields. We come so near,
so far, grounded as we are—
ninety miles apart as the crow flies,
a hundred million miles from the sun.

3.10

Brutal, the euphorbia thinks, feet puddled
since early January then in marched March
with no real idea in its greeny fists beyond
how weather works. Et tu? One morning—
elation!—two cereal bowls. Fifteen-
hundred later, you just want the answer
to 42-across *(shank in San Quentin)* sans
jibber-jabber and pileups. All signs point to
another close shave in the shower. A muddle,
this middle. Brittle. We came—now we see
all the hats in the house have been conquered.

So, let's recap. The last act we discovered a body
contains enough iron to make a paper clip
though not a surgical staple much less a complete
setting for six. Ever since, we've sung hymns
to unbury ourselves. Spurge quivers—go figure.
But look here: a mere two alpha-bits sit between
a malevolent spoon and small swoon of delight.
Chance of rain, says the riverside radio, *possibly changing
to rain overnight*. Sudden burst *(synonym for not-red
light)*—you pick up a pen. Well, then. All right.

THE HUMAN BODY

is two-thirds water, one-third
hydroelectric dam—with a lady in a barrel going over the falls.

The body is equal quarters
Okefenokee, albino catfish, caiman smile, ball
python coiled in the sink. A cypress takes root in the colon.

Today I am one-eighth
out of breath, three-fifths enlarged heart, finished
in medulla oblongata. Yesterday I was all guts.

My body is half
Wakatomika River, half white iris, half
blackhand sandstone—it doesn't add up.

You are part Gulf Stream, part Mississippi muck. Oyster bed. Rake.
The body is silica. It burns—it is briefly
Lalique. Your late-night body
is mixed signals and static, Muddy
Waters, magnetic bliss.

Your body names me in Braille. I tattoo your divides
with my tongue. You wrap me in your mother's
forty-grit-soul-scrub towels, you carry me
to shore, I carry you away, but our bodies remain

the last rest stop on the West Virginia turnpike
where the water fountain works but smells of pulp,
slag, silt. The body is our toll, our penny souvenir.
It's the map we can't refold: You are here.

NOTES

"And When I Hear That Voice I Feel a Great Joy" takes its title from Joan of Arc's 1429 testimony, as translated by Willard Trask.

"Rehearsal Notes for Adoptive Mother" takes its subtitles from Samuel Beckett (*Ghost Trio, Not I, Act Without Words,* and *Come and Go*) and quotes Emily Dickinson [405].

"Forgetting May Be Part of the Process of Remembering" takes its title from an article that appeared in the June 5, 2007, *New York Times*, in which the phrase "inhibiting the encroachment" also occurs.

The title "Put Thou My Tears into Thy Bottle" references Psalm 56.

ACKNOWLEDGMENTS

Abundant thanks to the editors of the following journals for selecting my poems (some in earlier versions) for publication:

AGNI: "We End, Like Galileo" (as "Galileo in Florence")
The Alembic (Providence College): "Licking County: 1931"
Born: "Physical Law"
The Burnside Review: "The Past in Thirteen Presents"
Caffeine Destiny: "Most Accidents Occur at Home" and "Winging It"
Field: "Hunger" and "Margin of Error"
Fireweed: "Solo," "Field Notes on the Family" (as "Suburban Field Notes"), and "Revisionary"
Jacket: "One More Name You Won't Associate with Water"
Orion: "We Bring the Wrong Tools"
Poetry Northwest: "New Math" and "The Human Body"
The Seattle Review: "Like This, Only More So," "Spring Comes to the Mistress of the Obvious," and "Images in Answer to Biology"
The Sow's Ear Poetry Review: "The First Time Your Daughter Runs Away from Home" (later published in *Fireweed*)
Talking River Review: "Apiary"
Tin House: "After a Fashion" (later published in *Born*), "Absent-minded," and "Put Thou My Tears into Thy Bottle" (as "Remembering")
Willow Springs: "No. 2 Venus"

Many thanks also to Oregon Literary Arts and to Soapstone for providing support when I most needed it.